THE BASICS OF
WINNING
CHESS

Jacob Cantrell

- Gambling Research Institute -
Cardoza Publishing

Cardoza Publishing, publisher of **Gambling Research Institute** (GRI) books, is the foremost gaming and gambling publisher in the world with a library of more than 50 up-to-date and easy-to-read books and strategies.

These authoritative works are written by the top experts in their fields and with more than 3,500,000 books in print, represent the best-selling and most popular gaming books anywhere.

Printing History

First Printing	*February 1989*
Second Printing	*March 1990*

New Revised Edition

First Printing	*January 1993*
Second Printing	*April 1994*

ISBN:0-940685-28-0
Library of Congress Catalogue Card Number: 92-70773

Cover Photo by Ron Charles

CARDOZA PUBLISHING
P.O. Box 1500, Cooper Station, New York, NY 10276
(718)743-5229

Table of Contents

Diagrams

I. Introduction

Chess is a game that combines artistry and pure skill. There is absolutely no luck involved in play, and while it is a game that can be easily learned, the profundities involved can last a lifetime of study. This is meant as a compliment to the game, not a deterrent to its understanding.

Chess is at once simple and complex and has intrigued millions of players throughout the world for centuries, as I am sure it will intrigue you, the reader. And there is nothing as rewarding as playing a fine game of chess, of making a few beautiful moves, or combinations, and defeating an opponent, whether that opponent be a human being or computer.

Chess can be played at various levels. One can play against other players in the privacy of one's home, or in a local chess club, of which there are thousands across America, and play others of like skill. As one improves, there are many tournaments available for the novice and more skilled player. Chess can even be played alone, against a computer.

Welcome to the greatest game ever invented by man, a game of profound beauty and lasting intrigue, a game that has enchanted and intrigued millions and should do the same for you - chess!

II. The Fundamentals of Chess

The Players

Two players battle against each other in chess; one handling the white pieces and the other the black pieces. The first player is designated as **White,** the second, as **Black.** Between the two players is the chessboard.

The Chessboard

The **chessboard** is a perfect square, consisting of 64 smaller squares that alternate in color, dark and light. To set up the chessboard correctly, the lower right hand corner should always be a white square. Looking at the board, we see that it is divided into

horizontal and vertical rows. Each horizontal row is called a **rank;** each vertical row, a **file.**

In the game itself, pieces, depending on their particular scope, can move not only along the ranks and files, but may also move diagonally on the chessboard.

The Pieces and Pawns

The game is played with chess pieces, also called either men or chessmen, and pawns, a total of 32 in all, 16 for each side. Each player, black and white, has eight pawns ♟ , two rooks ♜ , two knights ♞ , two bishops ♝ , one queen ♛ , and one king ♚ .

The next illustration shows the positions of the chessmen and pawns on the board at the outset of the game, before the first move is made. To verify the correctness of the position of the pieces, always remember that the queen of each side is always on its own color; i.e. the white queen is on a white square and the black queen on a black square.

Pawns

There are eight pawns on each side, and they occupy the entire second rank. A pawn can move forward either one or two squares on its initial move; thereafter, it can advance only one rank forward at a time.

We suggest you set up the chess pieces as in the previous diagram, and move the pawn in front of the white king's bishop. Advance it two spaces. Now advance the black pawn in the same file, the black king's bishop pawn, also two ranks. By doing this, we now have the white and black pawns on the same file as follows:

Neither pawn can now move. Since the pawns are abutting each other on the same File, they are said to be **blockaded,** for a pawn cannot move backwards at any time.

In the following diagram, we see one of the two situations where a pawn can **take** another pawn or piece, and that is by moving diagonally forward one square.

If it is the white pawn's turn to move, it could take off the black pawn by moving into the square that the black pawn occupies. If it were the black pawn's turn to move, it could take off the white pawn by moving into the square that the white pawn occupies. Once a pawn or piece is taken, it goes off the board and is removed from play.

There is one other way that a pawn can capture another pawn. It is called **en passant.** If a white pawn, for example, is on the fifth rank, and the black pawn advances on an adjacent file by moving up two ranks or its initial move, it can be taken off by the white pawn, *en passant.* To illustrate, move one of your pawns to the fifth rank on the chessboard. Now move an enemy pawn (of the opposite color) two ranks forward on an adjacent file. To take off the enemy pawn, the first pawn moves into the other pawn's file on its sixth rank. Now, the first pawn is on the sixth rank in the same file previously occupied by the enemy pawn.

Pawns get more powerful as other pieces are removed from the board since they have the power of **queening** in the endgame. If a pawn can advance to the eighth or last rank, it can be exchanged for any other piece. Thus, a lowly pawn can be made into a queen, the most powerful offensive piece on the board. Or it can be exchanged for any other piece, except a king, if the player so wishes.

This fluidity of pieces makes chess so very fascinating. The lowly pawn, now a passed pawn, with no enemy pawn on its file blocking the way, and heading for the eighth rank to be queened, often determines all the strategy of play in an **endgame,** that part of a chess game where most of the pieces have been removed, and only a king, pawns and perhaps a piece or two remain on the board.

The Rook

The rook is sometimes called a castle, with the symbol R, for rook. Each side has two rooks, and their position on the board is at the edge, in the last files on the first rank.

A rook can only move in straight lines, either on a rank or file. The next diagram illustrates this:

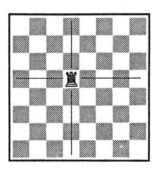

A rook can move straight on any file or rank the full length of the board, as long as the rank or file is open. However, a rook can, like all other pieces except for the knight, be blockaded by its own men or an enemy piece or pawn. If it is blockaded by its own men, it cannot move further forward, either on a rank or file. If it is blockaded by an opposing (enemy) pawn or piece, it can move into that enemy's square and take off the pawn or piece.

A rook's great strength is in controlling a whole file even from its first rank position. It is a powerful offensive piece, ranked next to the queen in strength.

The Bishop

The bishops, like the rooks, come in pairs. However, the bishops move only on diagonals, rather than in straight lines. Each side has one bishop that controls the white squares, and another bishop that controls the black squares. When, in the course of a game, there remains only one bishop on each side, and each controls different colored diagonals, they are said to be *"bishops of opposite colors."*

Like the rook, the bishop can be blockaded by its own or enemy men or pawns, and can remove an enemy piece or pawn that is in the diagonal that the bishop covers by moving into its square.

The following diagram shows the movements of the bishop:

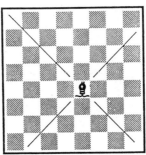

Often, a single bishop remaining in the game determines the tactics of the players. For example, if white has only one bishop remaining, and it controls the black or dark squares of the chessboard, but the black pawn which is trying to queen will arrive at the eighth rank on a white or light square, the bishop may be useless in stopping the queening of the pawn.

In terms of offensive power, the bishop ranks below the queen and the rook.

The Queen

The queen is the most powerful of all the pieces in chess. Each side has only one queen, and it combines the moves of the rook and bishop, and can move, like both other pieces, from one end of the board to the other, if the file, rank or diagonal is open. If a piece or pawn of its own color is in the way, it will be blockaded. However, if an opposing piece or pawn is in the way, it can be taken by the queen.

The following diagram shows all the possible moves of the queen:

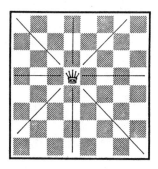

The queen can take off enemy pieces or pawns on diagonals, files or ranks, and this gives it enormous offensive power. Since it is so powerful, it is best that the queen be considered and used as a heavy artillery piece, staying in the rear and wreaking its havoc by controlling a diagonal, file or rank. When it is moved to the front, it may be under attack. Often, weak or inexperienced players move the queen too soon, and then spend half the game wasting moves with the queen, as it stays under constant attack.

The King

Each side has only one king. The king can make all the moves the queen can make, either straight or on any diagonal. However, the king can only move one square at a time, and thus its movements are limited. The following diagram illustrates the movement of the king:

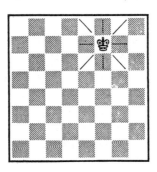

The limited mobility of the king makes him subject to attack. The purpose of the game of chess is to attack and capture the enemy or opposing king. If this is done, the game is over. Any other piece or pawn removed from the game doesn't end it, but the removal of the king ends the game.

By the rules of chess, if an enemy king is subject to immediate capture or removal, that is, *"in take,"* then the player attacking the king must warn the opposing player of this by announcing **"check."** If any other piece or pawn is under attack, no warning need be given.

When a king is under attack, and cannot escape capture and removal, then the opposing player simply announces **"checkmate,"** signifying that the king cannot escape. The following position shows a checkmate:

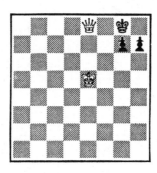

The white queen has just moved to the eighth rank and checkmated the black king. No matter where the king moves, it can be taken by the queen, so it is checkmate and the game is over.

The king cannot move into a capturing position. If it is so moved, the other player must point this out, so that the move can be retracted.

The Knight

The knight goes under two symbols, either Kn or N. The more common symbol these days is N, for Kn is often mixed up with the symbol for the king, which is K.

In two ways, the knight is a unique piece. First of all, it can move over standing men in its way, and thus it can't be blockaded the way other pieces or pawns can. For example, on the first move, the knight can go over the knight's pawn, and advance to the third rank.

Secondly, the knight moves neither straight or on a diagonal. It moves in an L-shape, that is, one forward and two to the side, or two forward and one to the side. In the following diagram, the knight can land on the squares of any of the pawns on the board, and thus remove any of them.

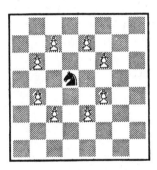

However, the knight cannot capture pieces or pawns it passes over in the process of making a move. It can only capture an enemy piece or pawn in the square it lands on.

Symbols of the Pieces

Remember, each piece has a particular symbol used in notations. While some books show the pieces themselves as symbols, the following are standard:

King = K, Queen = Q, Rook = R, Bishop = B, Knight = Kn or N. The pawn in the English notations is P, but has no designated letter in the Algebraic system, being dealt with differently there. We will use these symbols in all our future notations in this work.

Castling

Since the king is so important and his safety is of prime strategical consideration, the rules of chess allow castling, which puts the king in a position of great safety. It can be done by either player, and can be done on either side of the board; the king's side (where the king stands) or the queen's side (where the queen stands).

Castling involves moving the king and either the queen's rook or the king's rook, depending upon the side one is castling on, and must meet the following criteria:

First of all, neither the rook nor the king can have moved previously. Secondly, no pieces can stand between the king and the rook. Third, no enemy piece or pawn can be attacking the spaces between the king and rook on the first rank. Fourth, it must be that side's turn to move, for castling counts as a single move. And last, the king cannot be in check.

Let's now assume that the king and the king's rook (the rook closest to the king) haven't moved, and there are no pieces between them, for the bishop and knight on the king's side have previously moved out of the first rank. Let's further assume that no enemy pieces or pawns are attacking the spaces on the first rank between the king and rook and that the king is not in check.

Now we are able to castle. We do this by moving the king two spaces toward the rook, and then we move the rook two spaces away from the end or first file toward the king and around it, so that it now is on the other side of the king. That is **king-side castling.**

We can castle on the other side, called **queenside castling,** if the same five principles are met. To castle **long,** as this is also called, we move the king two spaces towards the rook, and then move the rook three spaces toward the king, so that it is now on the other side of the king on the first rank. In the following illustration, the white king has castled on the kingside, while the black king has castled on the queenside. Note the positions of the kings and rooks, and reread the above to be perfectly clear as to how one castles.

The notation used for castling is as follows:
King-side castling = 0-0
Queen-side castling = 0-0-0

III. Additional Rules of Play

1. White always makes the first opening move, and then black moves, and thereafter each side alternates with one move apiece.

2. The object of the game is to capture the opposing king, known as **checkmate.** Once he is captured, the game is over. A player who puts the opposing king in take must announce this by saying **"check."**

3. A player shouldn't wait for his king to be captured to lose the game if his position is hopeless. Often beginners lose piece after piece and still play on. If you have a lost position, you can **resign.** You resign by announcing your resignation or tipping over your own king. Most tournament games end in resignation, rather than checkmate.

4. A piece or pawn is captured when the opposing piece or pawn moves into its square. After a piece or pawn is so captured, it is taken off the board and removed from play.

5. A pawn that reaches the eighth rank must be replaced by another piece, other than a king. Usually it is replaced by a queen. This is called queening, or pawn promotion.

6. A game may be **drawn,** or tied, under the following circumstances:

    a. Both parties agree by mutual consent.

    b. There are insufficient pieces on the board to force checkmate. For example, if one player has only a king remaining, and the other has but a knight or bishop and a king, then checkmate is impossible. There are other examples of *book draws,* which we won't go into here.

    c. Perpetual check ends the game in a draw. If one side can perpetually check the opponent's king, and does so to force a draw, the game is over.

    d. Repetition of the identical position for any three times during the game ends in a draw. This prevents constant stalling by one side.

    e. **Stalemate** causes a draw. In this case, the king is the only piece that can make a legitimate move, and it's only move is into check. Since a king can't move into check, it is a stalemate.

    f. If, in fifty consecutive moves, there has been no capture or no pawn has moved, it is a drawn game.

(Some of the above rules are complicated, and only experience in chess will make them clearer. Don't worry about them too much. Most games end in resignation or checkmate).

7. In private games, there is usually no time limit to the number of moves that can be made. However, in tournament play, a chess clock is used, and each player has a predetermined amount of time to make all his moves. If he can't make his moves within that time frame, he loses the game.

8. If a player touches a piece or pawn, he is obligated to move that piece or pawn. If he touches several pieces or pawns, the opponent can choose which piece or pawn should be moved. For beginners, this is important. Learn to play patiently, and don't touch any piece or pawn until you're sure you want to move it.

A player may adjust his pieces or pawns, however, without penalty. The usual phrase, said beforehand, is *"J'adoube,"* or *"I adjust."*

9. If you decide to play that touching is not automatically a move, then the following should go into effect. If a player moves a piece or pawn and takes his or her hand off it, the move is complete and cannot be retracted.

10. If an illegal move is made by an opponent, he must retract it upon demand of the other player, and another legal move must be made by the same piece or pawn. If the illegal move was a capture, the capture must be made legally by another piece, if possible.

IV. Chess Notations

Notations are a method of recording the moves of any chess game played. Because of notations, not only can you and your opponent replay your own games, but players today can play and replay all the great games of the past, since all the world championships and practically all the great tournaments of the past have been notated.

Algebraic System

There are basically two types of notating systems. The most common today, and one that is used worldwide, is called the **Algebraic system.** It is very precise, and is used universally when computer chess is played.

The following diagram shows how a board is notated. Note that each file has a letter, running from the first file, which is a, to the last, which is h. And each rank has a number attached. The first rank is 1, and the last is 8. When a piece lands on c5, for example, there is no doubt on which square it has landed.

This is a clear way of notating and has pretty much replaced the older, English notation system. We'll also show that system later, because many early books are notated in the English system. But for now, let's look at a diagram of the chessboard showing the Algebraic system.

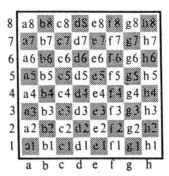

Let's now go over the symbols used in the Algebraic system. First, the pieces. K = king, Q = queen, R = rook, B = bishop and N = knight. The pawn is simply designated by its position on the board. So, let's now show the moves at the beginning of the game, usually called the **opening.** White moves first, and now moves the pawn in front of the king two spaces up. In all notations, white's moves are shown on the left, and black's on the right.

1. e4

What white had done in reality has been to move the pawn in front of the king from e2 to e4. We don't have to show this, merely the square where the pawn finally landed, which is e4.

Now black moves its king's pawn up two ranks.

1. e4   e5

The black pawn has moved from e7 to e5, but we only show its' final destination, the e5 square.

Let's continue the game for a few more moves, to show clearly what moves have taken place. Now it is white's turn to make it's second move.

1. e4   e5
2. Nf3

Although white has two knights, it can only move one to that square of f3, and that is the king's knight, which started on g1. It is now attacking the black pawn on e5, for it can take that pawn on the next move. Black now moves.

1. e4   e5
2. Nf3   Nc6

Black has now moved its own queens' knight from b8 to c6. Again, we only show the final destination of the piece, not where it moved from. Thus, the black knight, by moving, is now covering and protecting its e5 pawn from take by the white knight stationed on f3. If the white knight takes the pawn, it will be captured by the black knight, an unequal exchange.

Other Algebraic Notations

When a piece or pawn takes an enemy chessman, the notation for capture is x. Thus, if the queen captured a piece on g6, the notation would read as follows:

Qxg6

We don't have to show what piece or pawn was on g6, only the fact that whatever was there was taken off by the queen.

Checking a king is shown by a +. Thus, if the bishop moved to h6 and checked the king, the notation would show as follows:

Bh6+

If the same bishop had taken off a pawn at h6, the notation would show as follows;

Bxh6+

We will use the Algebraic system throughout the work as the standard system, and will also show the **English or Descriptive System** to clarify both possible notations.

English System

As we stated, this system is no longer the standard, but many works in chess literature have used it, and it is useful to know. In the following diagram, we see the board set up for this system:

Immediately, we can see that it is more complicated than the Algebraic system. For one thing, instead of letters for the various files, each file is designated by the piece that is on this file. And further, the numbers representing the ranks, run in two directrions. To illustrate how this system works, let's now show the same moves we described before with the Algebraic system.

The first move by white is the king's pawn moving up two ranks. Now this is notated as follows:

1. P-K4

Thus, we know that the king's pawn has moved up two ranks in the king's file. Black's reply of its own king's pawn moving up two spaces would now show as follows:

1. P-K4   P-K4

The black pawn has moved up to its own king's pawn 4 rank.

Now the white knight move:

1. P-K4   P-K4
2. N-KB3

The white king's knight has moved into the king's bishop's file, to the third rank. The reply by the black knight is as follows:

1. P-K4   P-K4
2. N-KB3   1-N-QB3

The black knight, to protect it's king's pawn, has moved into the third rank on the queen's bishop's rank.

The same symbols are used for the pieces, as in the Algebraic system, except that the pawn is designated as P. Also, sometimes the knight is designated as Kt as well as N.

The checking of the king is shown as ch, rather than as + in the Algebraic system. Thus, a queen taking a bishop and checking the king, would be shown as follows:

QxBch.

Here, in the English system, we don't show the square that the queen is checking from, and when a piece or pawn is taken, that symbol is used to show the piece or pawn taken. If a pawn takes a pawn, for example, it would be shown as PxP. A king taking a pawn would be shown as KxP.

Symbols Common to Both Systems

There are a number of symbols common to both the Algebraic and English systems. They are as follows:

Pawn takes pawn en passant = (e.p.)

A strong or best move = !

A brilliant move is = !!

A poor move is = ?

A losing move is = ??

A speculative move is = !? or ?!

To illustrate some of these, we show the following:

Qxc5!

Bxd4!!

Ne7??

Other common symbols are:

Kingside castling = 0-0

Queenside castling = 0-0-0

Notating a Game

In notating the next game, we're going to show the moves in Algebraic, but will also show the English system in parentheses, so that the reader will be able to follow the game under both systems.

Remember, white always moves first. The following game will have a heading, which is the title of the opening, the **Ruy Lopez.** Various openings are standard and have been named for decades or even hundreds of years. This is one of the ancient openings, still in use today. The two players, Alekhine as white, and Capablanca as black, were both world champions, and two of the greatest players in the history of the game.

The Ruy Lopez Opening

A. Alekhine   R. Capablanca

1. e4   (P-K4)   e5   (P-K4)

Both men have advanced their king pawns, which now have blockaded each other.

2. Nf3   (N-KB3)   Nc6   (N-QB3)

In this opening, white attacks the black center pawn with his knight, and black immediately defends it with his queen's knight.

3. Bb5   (B-N5)

The white bishop goes to the attack, threatening to take the black knight. This opening immediately puts pressure on the black pieces.

                                    a6   (P-Qr3)

Black's queen pawn, by moving up one rank, is now attacking the white bishop, since the pawn takes on a diagonal.

4. Ba4   (B-R4)

The bishop, which can only move on a diagonal, retreats to the safety of its own a4 square, still attacking the black knight.

                                    Nf6   (N-B3)

The other black knight comes out, attacking the white center pawn, which is undefended.

5. Nc3   (N-B3)

Now white brings out its own queen's knight, to protect its center pawn.

At this point, let's see what a diagram of the chessboard should look like after these moves.

We suggest that you make the moves on your own chessboard at the outset of this sample game, and then compare it to the above chessboard. If your board looks exactly like the diagrammed one, you've made the correct moves. If it differs, make your moves again carefully.

V. Principles of Play

The game of chess can be divided into three distinct parts, which are known as follows: *The Opening,* the *Middle Game* and the *End Game.* We'll cover the principles involved in each part of the game, starting with the opening.

Opening Principles

1. Open with your king or queen pawn if you are white, by moving either e4 or d4. The purpose of the above move is twofold: It allows you freedom to move one of your bishops into play, and it also moves to control the center.

The control of the center is very important in chess. It consists of the third to sixth ranks on the king and queen's files (d3-d6 or e3-e6). Without control of the center, the position quickly disintegrates. Sometimes more advanced players put off controlling the center to a later time, but as a beginner, make moves that control that vital area.

Often weak or beginning players move their rook pawns forward early, hoping to free the rook to come out. These are terrible moves, to be avoided. Rook pawns become targets of enemy pieces, and are best left on the first rank or eighth rank, depending on whether they are white or black. From there they control files, and can be used for castling.

2. Once having moved a center pawn, generally, you shouldn't move it again. Now develop your other pieces.

3. In developing pieces, the general rule is, knights before bishops. Put the knights on the third rank, either on the squares c3 or f3 if white, or c6 or f6 if black. From those posts they exert tremendous pressure on a large part of the chessboard. Many beginners post the knights at the edge of the board, on a3, for example, wasting most of the board, for at the edge, the knight's rule is limited. Knights can not only attack enemy pawns at the outset of play, but can also protect its own pawns.

The bishop, once it is moved off the back rank, controls diagonals in two separate directions, and becomes a powerful force.

4. The point in chess is to develop your pieces and get them off the back rank. However, don't be in a hurry to develop your two most powerful pieces, the queen and the pair or rooks. Develop the knights and bishops however, not only to get them into play, but also to clear the spaces between the rook and king so that castling is possible.

5. Don't delay castling too long. It is important to first protect your king, before going on the complete offensive, otherwise, the opponent may counterattack the undefended king. Once you've castled, you have another plus - your rooks now are in the center files, controlling them instead of the end files. And if the two rooks can be made to work in tandem, with no

pieces between them, they become much more powerful.

6. If you move the queen, use it as a threat or to back up the center or other pieces. Don't shove it to the middle of the board, where it may be under attack by enemy forces. If you do this, you'll be wasting precious moves protecting or moving the queen. And worse still, you may blunder and lose it. Losing the queen pretty much means your game is lost, unless you have adquate compensation for its loss, such as taking the opponent's queen or two rooks.

7. Don't make unnecessary moves at the beginning of the game. Post your pieces to protect the center or dominate the center. Once you've found a good outpost for a piece, develop other pieces. Don't move a piece twice without a really good reason.

8. Don't move pawns unless necessary, once you've moved the center pawns. Keep your pawn structure intact. Later on, a strong pawn structure is a tremendous asset, for it is difficult to attack without loss, and it can be used as an offensive weapon at the right time.

9. If you are white, try and keep the offensive. Don't give it up to black, or your game will have lost its whole purpose. White should have a lasting initiative. As black, you want to defend carefully and try to wrest the initiative from white at the appropriate time.

Middle Game Principles

After the pieces have been developed in the opening, and a number of moves made, the game flows into the middle game. There is no definite number of moves that have to be made before we're in the middle game, for these terms are rather fluid.

1. Keep your pieces co-ordinated, so that they can work together. Having pieces scattered all over the board only invites trouble. They can be attacked by the enemy, and without working together, your pieces cannot mount a solid offensive.

2. Having kept your rooks on the back rank, you now want to make sure they are most effective. Therefore, open files for them, so that they can control complete files. You do this by exchanging pawns and clearing up a file. Once you have an open file, strive to get your rook in position to control it.

3. Your bishops operate only on diagonals, one for the black and one for the lighter squares. Many times you'll find that one of your bishops have been exchanged by the middle game, or is about to be captured. If your remaining bishop controls light squares, keep them open so that the bishop can operate with maximum mobility. If you have a bishop controlling the dark squares, keep those squares open for fully mobility.

Conversely, blockade the opponent's bishop, so that it can't be effective, by shoving pawns in its way, or keep whatever diagonal it operates on blocked with pawns or pieces.

4. Knights, which should have been moved to the c and f files at the outset of play, should be kept in the center in the middle game, where they are most effective in attacking the enemy and protecting their own pieces. Avoid putting knights near the edge of the board at any time, except where there is a definite tactical reason or strategy for doing so - such as an attack that can only be done in that fashion.

5. If you find that you game is cramped, that is, your pieces are blockaded and you have little scope to move them, then your best tactic is to trade off some of the pieces or pawns, to free your game. For example, you might have a bishop blocked on its diagonal. Try and exchange this piece for an enemy bishop or knight.

On the other hand, if your enemy is cramped and you have mobility, try to avoid exchanging pieces. As he stays cramped, you go to the offensive.

6. If you are on the attack, try to avoid exchanges which will weaken your attack. For example, if you have two or three co-ordinated pieces bearing down on the enemy king's position, don't lose them through exchanges, for you may dissipate your attack completely.

7. If your enemy has weakened his pawn structure with unnecessary moves at the outset of play, or has **doubled** his pawns, having two in a file where they don't protect one another, attack this weakness. By forcing your opponent to bring his pieces to their defense, you may completely unbalance his game, and cause it to be a losing game. While you're attacking, he's wasting moves defending.

On the other hand, avoid weakening your own pawn structure. Keep it solid, and don't put holes in it, that is, a space between two pawns, which can open a file for the enemy rook or the posting of a bishop or knight by the enemy deep in your territory.

8. If you find a hole in your opponent's pawn structure, with such an open file, not only try and get your rook to control that file, but try and post a knight or bishop deep into his territory, guarded by your own pawn, where it is practically impossible to dislodge

33

him without loss on the part of your opponent, either in time or men.

9. If your opponent is susceptible to attack, then rip open his files so that your big pieces, your queen and rooks can bear down on his position.

10. If you have the lead in development of pieces, try to keep opening the position so that your attack will be successful. Conversely, if your opponent has the lead in development, try and close up the position, blockading his forces, so that his attack will be nullified.

11. If you are attacking on one wing, that is, one side of the board, make certain that your other wing is not susceptible to attack. Sometimes, before beginning such a wing attack, you want to make a move or two that protects your own side.

12. On the other hand, if you are being attacked on one wing, often the best counter-attack is to go after the other wing or the center. If possible, counterattck, or you will find the opponent bringing all his forces into play for his own attack. By mounting your own attack, you will cause him to divert pieces for his own self defense. In this strategy, chess is akin to actual war.

13. If you get ahead by a piece, then exchange as many pieces as you can, for the fewer pieces on the board, the greated your advantage with an extra piece. On the other hand, if a piece behind, try and conserve your remaining pieces.

14. If you're a pawn or two ahead, steer for the endgame where those extra pawns are awesome, by exchanging off the pieces. The fewer pieces on the board, the more powerful your extra pawns become.

15. Before moving, plan a few moves ahead of time. Try and think of the move your opponent will make to counter each of your moves. Think of several possibilities before moving. As the great Emmanuel Lasker, a former world champion, said, "If you see a good move, don't make it. There is always a better move to make."

End Game Principles

By the end game there are a few pieces left on either side, and now the pawns and the king come into play as strong offensive weapons.

1. The king can become a strong attacking weapon, even though it can only move one square at a time. With few big pieces on the board, it has more maneuverability. Try and work it to the center and into the enemy position, and co-ordinate its attack with your remaining pieces.

2. The pawns now reach their full potential in the end game. A **passed pawn** is awesome on the chessboard, and is a pawn on a file with no opponent's pawn in its way.

If you have a passed pawn, concentrate on getting it to the end rank where it can be queened. Protect and support it, for then you'll put tremendous pressure on your opponent to blockade it in whatever way he can.

3. Often, an opponent will have to sacrfice a piece to get rid of a passed pawn, by taking it off, or capturing a pawn supporting it. On the other hand, if your opponent has a passed pawn, you can't neglect it. You must take active measures to neutralize it, or if possible, to capture it.

4. Since the pawns in the endgame are so powerful, you want to avoid having doubled pawns, that is, two pawns of your own on one file, where they are subject to attack. Try and have pawns in adjacent files, where they can support one another.

Isolated pawns are weak as well. An **isolated pawn** is a pawn without any supporting pawn in an adjacent file. It can become a naked target for enemy pieces.

5. In rook and pawn endings, where rooks are the only pieces left on the board, get the rooks behind the pawns to protect them as they move toward queening, or if you have two rooks, try and get them deep into enemy territory. For example, if you have two rooks and are white, posting both rooks on the seventh rank will create havoc to the enemy position.

6. If you are ahead by a piece, keep exchanging. In the end game, your extra piece is usually all that is necessary for victory. If you're a piece behind, you must conserve what you have, and avoid exchanges at all costs.

7. However, if you are only one pawn ahead, don't exchange pawns. One pawn may not be enough to ensure your opponent's defeat. With two pawns to the good, exchange pawns. That will be enough for victory.

8. If behind in material, exchange the pawns. If you can get rid of the opponent's pawns, his one piece ahead may not be enough to defeat you. For example, without any pawns on the board, your king alone can't be checkmated by an opponent's king and knight, or king and bishop.

9. As you become more experienced, learn the basic mates and draws possible. Thus, you can go for mate

more easily, and if behind, you can steer the game into a draw, which is always more preferable than a loss.

10. In the end game, two bishops are more powerful than two knights, or one bishop and one knight. Because of their scope on the diagonals, the bishops will exert enormous power, especially with few pieces or pawns on the board to hinder their progress.

11. If there are many pawns left on the board, then a knight may have much more scope than a bishop in the end game, since the bishop's mobility will be restricted by pawns on its diagonal squares.

VI. Tactical Maneuvers

Chess is a game of tactics and strategy. There are some tactics that can be used by the aggressive, attacking player to great advantage. The following are some of these:

The Pin

A pin is a tactic used to freeze an opponent's piece so that it cannot be moved, either because moving it will cause the king to be captured, or will cause the loss of a major piece, such as a queen.

A pin has some advantages, the chief among them being the immobilization of the piece being pinned. In the next diagram, we see the white bishop pinning the black knight, which cannot move because it would mean the capture of the black king by the white bishop.

Discovered Check

This tactic creates havoc with the enemy pieces and often leads to the loss of material of consequence. It occurs when the piece that can check the king is blocked by another piece of the same color. The removal of the blocked piece to another square then puts the king in check. Either the king has to move, or another piece must be interposed between the opposing piece checking the king. In any case, the moved piece that caused the discovered check can go on to take material. This can be shown simply and clearly in the next diagram.

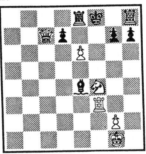

In the above illustration, it is white's turn to move. If he moves his knight, the rook will put the black king in check. If the white knight moves, for example, to the square d5, the black queen will be lost. The king has no piece to interpose, and must move out of check. It can of course interpose the bishop, but that can easily be taken with the same situation as before, since the black forces cannot retake the rook. After the black king moves out of check, to the square g8 (it cannot move to e7 because it would put itself into check because of the knight at d5) the white knight would take off the black queen.

Double Check

This tactic occurs when two pieces check the king at the same time. In the above illustration, suppose that the white knight moved to g6 instead of d5. Now both the knight and rook check the black king. The knight can't be taken by the pawn at h7, because the rook is also checking the black king.

The king is forced to move to g8. After this move, the white rook can move to f8, giving check. It must then be removed by the black rook at e8. Then the white knight, by moving to e7+ checkmates the black king. It has no escape hatch, for the white pawn at e6 stands in the way of the black knight moving to f7. A nice checkmate here!

Knight Fork

A knight always attacks a piece or pawn in a different colored square from the one it stands on. Thus, if a knight is on a dark square, it can only attack an opposing chessman that is on a white or light square.

Sometimes, if a knight is well-positioned, it can attack two enemy pieces at the same time, when both pieces are on the same colored square. When this happens, one of the pieces must be captured, for it cannot evade capture by the interposition of a piece between the knight and the piece to be captured. In the next illustration, we see that the knight is attacking both the king and queen at the same time. This is called a knight fork.

Since the king must move out of check, the queen will be lost to the white knight.

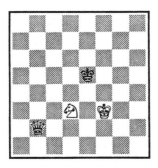

Combinations

Combinations can be said to be the "soul of chess." A combination is a series of moves, thought out in advance, in which several moves are forced on the defender, who has no choice in the matter, but which leads either to the defender's loss of material or mate.

Often these combinations involve the sacrifice of material by the attacker, and often the defender doesn't realize that in the end it will be he who will suffer, not the attacker.

The great players in history have all been masters of the combination, and it is one of the essential ingredients in any fine player's makeup. To see ahead, to plan several moves ahead, to sacrifice material for the purpose of winning the game - these traits are to be hailed. It is what separates the great from the good players. And it is a joy often to replay games in which combinations have wone the day.

In the following game played between two grandmasters, Hort of Czechoslovakia and Portisch of

Hungary, Hort, as white, is about to embark on a combination that will win the game for him.

As we follow the game from its 30th move, we see that Hort makes a series of moves, including sacrifices, which finally force black to lose the game. And like most combinations, this one seems to come out of the blue.

This is the position prior to the 30th move of white. Each side has equal pieces and pawns, but black has a hole in his position. The g file is open, and his f pawns are doubled up, breaking the chain between the h pawn and the f pawn. White now neatly exploits this weakness.

30.   Rg4+   (R-N4ch)

White is sacrificing his rook, forcing black to take it. Black cannot move his king - it has nowhere to hide, since the white queen holds the diagonal ending in h8.

                    fxRg4   (PxR)

31.   Qg5+   (Q-N5ch)

Now the black king must move, since it can interpose no piece between itself and the queen checking it.

                    Kh8   (K-R1)

This was the only move that black can now make.
32. Qh6!   (Q-R6)

Black resigned at this point rather than continuing in a lost cause. At this point, both the white queen and white bishop are attacking the h7 pawn, leading to instant mate if the white queen takes it. Black can defend it by moving his f pawn forward, thus permitting his queen to protect the h pawn. However, if he does this, then white will move 32. QxRf8, forcing mate this way. Since black can't defend both the h pawn and the rook at f8 at the same time, he resigns.

It is fascinating to read chess literature and to see the great masters make their combinations. Now that you know how the notation systems work, all of this literature is available for your study. It will not only entertain you, but give you insight into how the great masters think, and must, in this way, improve your game.

VII. Standard Openings

We wrote about opening principles before. Many of those principles have been incorporated into standard openings, a predetermined set of moves which characterize what is called a particular opening.

A beginning player will find a multitude of openings available to him. From these, he should cull a smaller number and study them. Eventually he will find openings that suit his own style of play. Some openings favor the attacking and aggressive player, while others favor players who are more interested in a slower, positional game, in which the pieces are well placed and small benefits lead to larger gains as the game progresses.

In this book, we'll cover a number of the standard openings used in chess today. Many of these are ancient and have stood the test of time. In grandmaster tournaments, played by the best players in the world, the first ten moves usually are made in a few seconds, since they are so standard, and known to all grandmasters.

Study and familiarize yourself not only with those openings suited to you play, but others as well, since you may be forced to defend against an opening as black that you wouldn't open as white.

As a beginner, we recommend that you know the following openings: Ruy Lopez, the Sicilian and French Defense as King Pawn's openings, and the Queen's Gambit and Queen's Indian among the Queen's Pawn openings. Then, once you've studied and mastered these, you can go on to other openings.

Openings are important because the moves they represent have stood the test of time as the best possible strategems available. Openings set the tone of the game and dictate which side will take the lasting initiative.

A. King's Pawn Openings: e4 (P-K4)

We will now deal with openings in which the first move is 1. e4 (P-K4)

Ruy Lopez

This is one of the oldest openings known and it is still widely used, since it gives the white player a lasting initiative at the outset of play. Recently, it has fallen in esteem to the Sicilian Opening, which we'll discuss next, since black tries to avoid the Ruy Lopez, and prefers an opening in which he doesn't have to cede the initiative immediately. In chess, remember, it takes two to tango!

The standard opening moves are:

1. e4	(P-K4)	e5	(P-K4)
2. Nf3	(N-KB3)	Nc6	(N-QB3)
3. Bb5	(B-N5)		

The most common variation of this opening is the Morphy Defense, which answers with 3 ...a6 (P-QR3)

Sicilian Defense

This defense is considered best these days for black, for it gives the black forces immediate counterplay, and isn't as passive as the Ruy Lopez for the defender.

The standard opening moves are:

1. e4	(P-K4)	c5	(P-QB4)
2. Nf3	(N-KB3)	d6	(P-Q4)
3. d4	(P-Q4)	cxd4	(PxP)
4. Nxd4	(NxQP)	Nf6	(N-KB3)

The above moves are common to the Najdorf and Dragon variations of the Sicilian. There are other variations known as the Taimonov, Paulsen and Scheveningen. We suggest that you study **Modern Chess Openings** as you become more involved with chess.

French Defense

Unlike the Sicilian, this is a quieter opening in which black tries to close up the position. It is best suited for non-aggressive players who prefer a solid, rather than an attacking defense.

The standard opening moves are:

1. e4	(P-K4)	e6	(P-K3)
2. d4	(P-Q4)	d5	(P-Q4)
3. Nc3	(N-QB3)	Nf6	(N-KB3)

There are two variations of the French that are popular - the Classical and the Winawer.

B. Queen's Pawn Openings: d4 (P-Q4)

For many years, the use of the queen's pawn as an opening move was considered inferior. However, today, most grandmasters and masters favor the use of d4 rather than e4 as the first move. This move also controls the center and easily develops the pieces of the white player. We highly recommend that the beginner study these openings as well as those that begin with 1. e4.

Queen's Gambit Declined

Although a pawn is sacrificed at the beginning in this opening, which gives it the term **gambit,** the sacrifice is temporary, for white easily regains the pawn. This opening is used extensively by modern masters.

The standard opening moves are:

1. d4	(P-Q4)	d5	(P-Q4)
2. c4	(P-QB4)	e6	(P-K3)
3. Nc3	(N-QB3)	Nf6	(N-KB3)
4. Bg5	(B-KN5)		

Variations of this opening are the Orthrodox, Exchange, Tarrasch and Ragozin. Also the Slav and Semi-Slav. Another variation is the Queen's Gambit Accepted, where, in Black's second move, it takes the pawn at c4 with its d pawn. Again, refer to **Modern Chess Openings.**

Queen's Indian Defense

The purpose of this opening is to control the center, particularly the square e4, with both black's queen's bishop and king's knight. To do this, black fianchettos on his queen's side. A **financhetto** is the movement of the bishop to the b7 square, where it controls the long diagonal leading to the white king's position.

The standard opening moves are:

1. d4	(P-Q4)	Nf6	(N-KB3)
2. c4	(P-QB4)	e6	(P-K3)

3. Nf3	(N-KB3)	b6	(P-QN3)
4. g3	(P-KN3)	Bb7	(-N2)
5. Bg2	(B-N2)	Be7	(B-K2)
6. 0-0			

There are analogous systems based on the Indian defense, known as the Nimzo-Indian and King's Indian.

Some other modern Queen's openings are the Modern Benoni and the Grunfeld Defense. What is important is to know some of the more popular openings used today, and then to go into further study of the variations. Combining this with the opening principles outlined in this work will make you into a competent player rather quickly.

VIII. Representative Games

We're going to show a few games played between grandmasters, so that you can replay the game yourself, using your pieces and your chess board.

Study how the grandmasters open their games and develop their pieces, and then follow their moves to the end. This is the best way, outside of actual chess play, to improve your game.

Game 1

Queen's Indian Defense

	Anatoly Karpov		Boris Spassky	
1.	d4	(P-Q4)	Nf6	(N-KB3)
2.	c4	(P-QB4)	e6	(P-K3)
3.	NF3	(N-KB3)	b6	(P-QN3)
4.	g3	(P-KN3)	Bb7	(B-N2)
5.	Bg2	(B-N2)	Be7	(B-K2)
6.	Nc3	(N-B3)	0-0	
7.	Qc2	(Q-B2)	d5	(P-Q4)
8.	cxd5	(PxP)	Nxd5	(NxP)
9.	0-0			

9...		Nd7	(N-Q2)
10.	NxNd5 (NxN)	exNd5	(PxN)
11.	Rd1 (R-Q1)	Nf6	(N-B3)
12.	Ne5 (N-K5)	c5	(P-B4)
13.	dxc5 (PxP)	Bxc5	(BxP)
14.	Nd3 (N-Q3)	Bd6	(B-Q3)
15.	Bf4 (B-B4)	Re8	(RpK1)
16.	e3 (P-K3)	Ne4	(N-K5)
17.	BxBd6 (BxB)	QxBd6	(QxB)
18.	Nf4 (N-B4)	Ra8c8?	(QR-B1)

(18... Qe5 is preferable here for black)

19. Qa4!

Now white threatens either BxNe4 or Oxa7.

19...		Qe7	(Q-K2)
20.	Qxa7 (QxP)	Nxf2	(NxBP)
21.	Nxd5 (NxP)	Bxnd5	(BxN)
22.	QxQe7 (QxQ)		

22...		NxRd1!? (NxR)

Black should have taken the white queen with his rook.

23. Rc1!

The white queen is now immune from capture. If it is taken, then RxRc8 and mate in two.

23...		Rb8	(R-N1)
24. Qb4	(Q-N4)	BxBg2	(BxB)
25. KxBg2	(KxB)	Nxe3+	(NxPch)
26. Kg1	(K-N1)	Re6	(R-K3)
27. Qf4	(Q-KB4)	Rd8?	(R-Q1)
28. Qd4!			

Again the queen is immune from capture because of the threat Rc8+ and mate in two.

28...		Rd8e8	(QR-K1)
29. Qd7	(Q-Q7)	Ng4	(N-N5)
30. Rc8	(R-B8)	Nf6	(N-B3)
31. RxR+	(RxRch)	RxR	(RxR)
32. Qb7	(Q-N7)	Re6	(R-K3)
33. Qb8+	(Q-N8ch)	Ne8	(N-K1)
34. a4	(P-R4)	g6	(P-N3)
35. b4	(P-QN4)	Kg7	(K-N2)
36. Qb7	(Q-N7)	h5	(P-R4)
37. h3	(P-R3)	Kf6	(K-B3)

38. Kg2 (K-N2)	Rd6 (R-Q3)
39. a5 (P-R5)	bxa5 (PxP)
40. bxa5 (PxP)	Re5 (R-K4)
41. a6 (P-R6)	Nc7 (N-B2)
42. a7! (P-R7)	

If the white queen had taken off the knight, then rook
would take pawn, and the ending would be problemati-
cal for white. Now the threat is queen takes knight, with
the additional threat of the pawn queening.

42...	Re7 (R-K2)
43. Qc6+ (Q-B6ch)	Kd5 (K-K4)
44. Kf3!	Resigns

Black resigns due to the fact that he is in *zugzwang*,
a German term meaning that he has no moves to make
that would not cost him a piece or the game. If the knight
moves, the pawn queens. If the rook moves, the knight
is lost. And so forth.

Game 2
Sicilian Defense

Robert Fischer		**Tigran Petrosian**	
1. e4 (P-K4)		c5 (P-QB4)
2. Nf3 (N-KB3)		e6 (P-K3)
3. d4 (P-Q4)		cxd4 (PxP)
4. Nxd4 (Nxp)		a6 (P-QR3)
5. Bd3 (B-Q3)		Nc6 (N-QB3)
6. NxN (NxN)		bxN (NPxN)
7. 0-0		d5 (P-Q4)
8. c4 (P-QB4)		Nf6 (N-B3)

52

9.	cxd5	(BPxP)		exd5	(KPxP)
10.	exd5	(PxP)		cxd5?	(PxP)

(10... QxP or NxP was better for black.)

| 11. | Nc3 | (N-B3) | | Be7 | (B-K2) |

12. Qa4+! (Q-R4ch)

Suddenly, black's game is thrown out of kilter by this move.

| 12... | | | | Qd7 | (Q-Q2) |

Black now is willing to sacrifice the exchange. White can move Bb5, with axB, and QxR, with black losing a rook for a bishop. But white declines with his next move.

13.	Rel	(R-K1)		QxQ	(QxQ)
14.	NxQ	(NxQ)		Be6	(B-K3)
15.	Be3	(B-K3)		0-0	
16.	Bc5!	(B-Qb5)		Rgel	(R-K1)
17.	BxB	(BxB)		RxB	(RxB)
18.	b4	(P-QN4)		Kf8	(K-B1)
19.	Nc5	(N-B5)		Bc8	(B-B1)
20.	f3	(P-B3)			

20...		Re7a7	(R(K2)-R2)
21.	Re5 (R-K5)	Bd7	(B-Q2)
22.	NxB+!(NxBch)	RxN	(RxN)
23.	Rc1 (R-QB1)	Rd6	(R-Q3)
24.	Rc7 (R-B7)	Nd7	(N-Q2)
25.	Re2 (R-K2)	g6	(P-N3)
26.	Kf2 (K-B2)	h5	(P-R4)
27.	f4 (P-B4)	h4	(P-R5)
28.	Kf3 (K-B3)	f5	(P-B4)
29.	Ke3! (K-K3)	d4+	(P-Q5ch)
30.	Kd2 (K-Q2)	Nb6	(N-N3)
31.	Re2e7 (R(K2)-K7)	Nd5	(N-Q4)
32.	Rf7+ (R-B7ch)	Ke8	(K-K1)
33.	Rb7 (R(QB7)-N7	Nxf4	(NxBP)
34.	Bc4	Resigns	

   With both white rooks on the seventh rank, and myriad threats all over the board, Petrosian decided to throw in the towel against the greatest player in the history of chess.

IX. The Chess Clock

The Element of Time

Most beginners and amateurs don't use a chess clock when playing among themselves. Time is therefore not a factor, but tournament and match play requires the use of a chess clock.

Time becomes very important, and a player can lose not only by resigning or being checkmated, but by running out of time.

Often, when I annotated games between grandmasters and found one player making blunders at the end, I realized he was under extreme time pressure and couldn't figure out the correct moves. He was fighting the clock as well as his opponent.

In modern tournaments the usual time limit is 40 moves in two and a half hours. That is, each player has two and half hours to make his own moves, and doubling that, the game can run to five hours for both players without exceeding the time limit.

To a beginner, that seems like an awfully long time, since amateur games played without a clock usually are resolved much before that.

But strong players facing equally strong players have to spend a lot of time figuring out all the possible variations, and the stronger the players, the more time they need.

We suggest that you purchase a chess clock, and use time as a factor in your games. You don't have to set such a long time limit, perhaps an hour to make forty moves would be sufficient.

If nothing else, it would prevent a player from just sitting there, or as the Germans say, exercising his *sitzfleish*, roughly translated as his "sitting flesh." A player who procrastinates for a half hour on a move can ruin any game, and the clock will prevent this.

Types of Chess Clocks

There are several kinds of clocks to choose from.

The older models, still in use and still very good, are the usual displays we see on watches and clocks, except that there are two bottoms. Each player has a button that when pressed down, activates the other player's clock. The button is pushed down after a player makes his move. Until then, his own clock is running.

These clocks have flags, which are activated during the last couple of minutes. When the flag rises as

56

the clock hand moves it up, time is very short. When the flag falls, the player has used up his time.

The other basic chess clocks are digitally run, and the time is shown just as it is on digital clocks, with the time decreasing as the game goes on. When the time moves to zero the game is over, for one player's time has expired.

X. Five Minute Chess

Introduction

Five minute chess requires a chess clock. Each player sets his time at five minutes, and must complete his moves within that time frame. Thus, the entire game can't take more than ten minutes.

Unlike ordinary chess, where, after the five hour period, if both players have made their 40 moves, the clocks are reset, in five minute chess, there's no resetting of clocks.

A player has three ways to win in five minute chess. He can **checkmate** the opponent's king, he can have the opponent **resign**, or the opponent can **run out of time**.

As soon as a player makes a move, he pushes his button down and the other player's clock is activated.

At the outset of play, the white pieces will move first. As soon as the first move is made, the player holding White pushes his button. Then it's the Black pieces turn to play. After his move, he pushes down the button, and so forth.

Special Five Minute Rules

There are two rules that are suspended in five minute chess. First, a player can touch a piece and not move it. There is intense time pressure and by taking back a move he's just wasting his time, which is precious. Secondly, if a king is in check, a player doesn't have to announce this.

If the opponent overlooks the fact that his king can be taken, and makes any other move, other than preventing checkmates, you can remove his king and he will lose at that point.

Five Minute Chess Strategy

Needless to say, in five minute chess, there is little time to think out complicated variations. You've got to move and move quickly, and not waste time.

To do this, what you want to do is study openings, such as the ones shown in this book, so that you know them by heart. You want to have several variations of these openings also committed to memory, so that you can improvise if the opponent doesn't follow the openings exactly or doesn't know them. This kind of preparation will help you enormously.

Above all, you want the clock on your side, and to do this, your opponent must stop and think about moves. You should complicate the game, or make more aggressive moves in five minute chess than you would ordinarily.

King side attacks are often very effective, since your opponent knows you don't have to call "check," and he has to carefully guard his king. All this takes time.

We highly recommend five minute chess as a terrific pastime. It's exciting and by moving fast, you get to learn how to think about chess in a wholly different way, which will help you in regular chess games.

IX. Afterword

Chess is a game of great beauty, and like all beautiful things, bears careful study. It constantly has surprises, and even the greatest players are always learning something new.

We suggest that you dip into the literature of chess and study the games of the great masters and champions of the past and present. Play out their games and study them carefully, for it will give you great dividends in your own play.

Chess is the pure game of skill - no luck is involved. The more skillful you become, the more you will enjoy and derive pleasure from chess.

We have given you enough information in this book to make you a fairly strong player at chess, so that you can play the greatest game ever invented, with pleasure and skill.

60

KASPAROV OLYMPIAD™
Chess Laptop for Beginning to Intermediate Players

GIVES YOU CHANCE TO BEAT THE COMPUTER
Saitek's first-ever **laptop chess computer** features **fun levels** where it actually makes some very real human errors. Even beginners have a chance to win! Convenient, economic and **powerful** (8K program), the Kasparov Olympiad™ has **outstanding features** including large sensory chessboard and info-packed LCD; beginning to intermediate players will be challenged by realistic play.

GREAT FOR HOME PLAY OR TRAVEL
The Olympiad is sleek and **ergonomically designed** and comes equipped with **two sets** of chess pieces; flat magnetic ones, **perfect for travelling**, and Staunton-style regular pieces for **play at home**. Includes built-in storage and travel cover.

64 LEVELS OF PLAY
64 levels of play makes an unbeatable choice for **beginning** and **intermediate** players. Improve level by level. As you become a better player, switch to more challenging levels. There's **problem-solving** and **coaching levels** which shows when pieces are threatened; solves up to mate-in-4. Includes most major openings in its library.

VERSATILE FEATURES
Knows all common chess rules and has features like 6 full move take-backs, automatic rejects of illegal moves, and on/off memory capabilitiy. Simply turn off game, and days later resume play - the Olympiad remembers the position for up to 18 months! Large LCD screen shows chess pieces, moves, set-up, checks, take-backs, depth of season, mate and draw status.
To order, send just $99.95 for the Kasparov Olympiad™

KASPAROV CHESS GK2000™
Saitek's Highest-Rated Tabletop Game

TOP OF THE RANGE - This **fabulous** chess computer has outstanding features and is the most popular one we sell. It's **high speed** program combined with **ease-of-use** and **top-notch** advanced technology brings consistent challenges and excitement. Rated at a **2100** ELO Performance. Uses **RISC** computer chip!
POWERFUL FEATURES - 64 levels of play include **sudden death, tournament**, and **beginner's**. Shows **intended move** and **position evaluation**, take back up to 30 ply, user selectable **book openings library**: choose from **Active, Passive, Tournament, complete book, no book**. Choose between high speed **Selective Search** or powerful **Brute Force** program. Thinks in opponents time. Shutoff, shut on memory. Remembers game for months!
GREAT TABLE-TOP DESIGN - Modern ergonomic design goes well in living room; **large LCD** shows **full information**, keeps track of playing time.
To order, send $199.95 for the Kasparov Chess GK2000.